Nintendo

3
Nintendo
ADVENTURE BOOKS
FEATURING THE SUPER MARIO BROS.
MONSTER MIX-UP

4
Nintendo
ADVENTURE BOOKS
FEATURING THE SUPER MARIO BROS.
KOOPA CAPERS

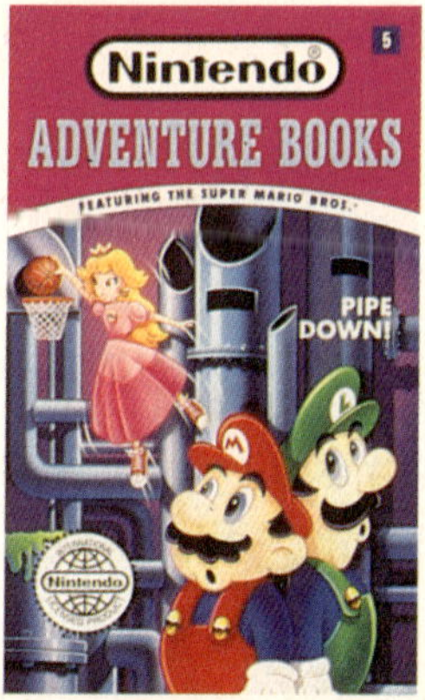
5
Nintendo
ADVENTURE BOOKS
FEATURING THE SUPER MARIO BROS.
PIPE DOWN!

6
Nintendo
ADVENTURE BOOKS
FEATURING THE SUPER MARIO BROS.
DOORS TO DOOM

Nintendo

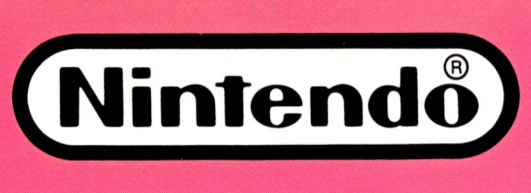

11

ADVENTURE BOOKS

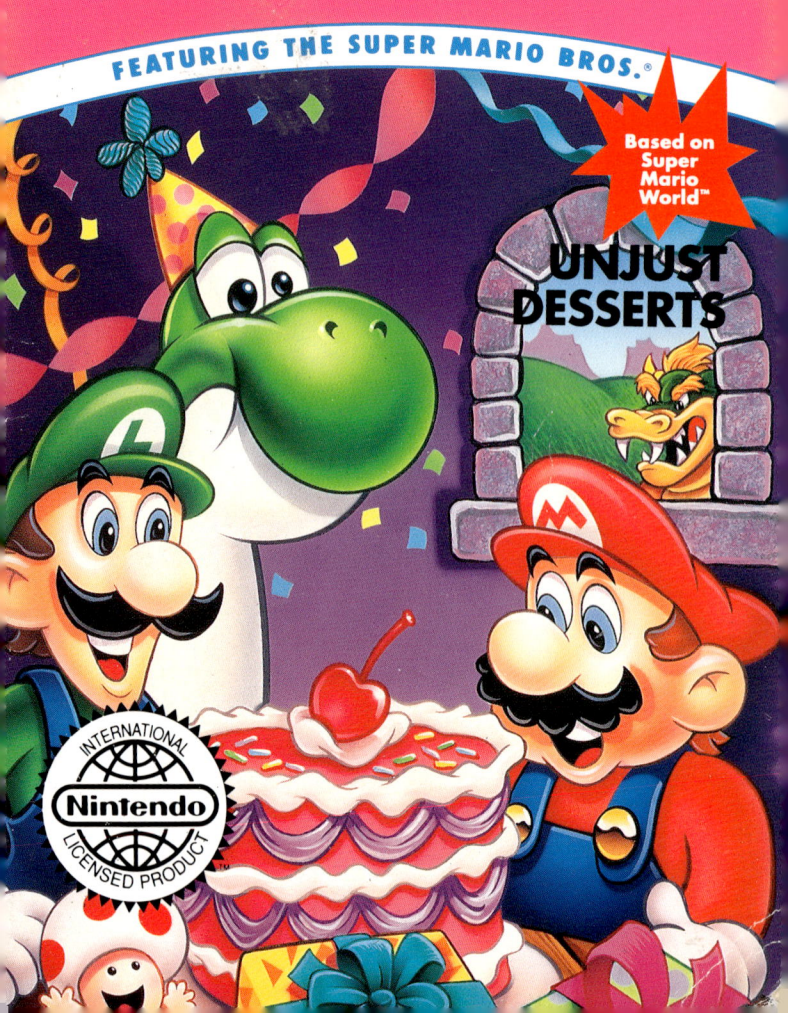

FEATURING THE SUPER MARIO BROS.

Based on Super Mario World

UNJUST DESSERTS

Internal Affair

"Yow!" shouts Mario. "What's that?"

The shrunken plumber thinks a giant pink mountain is about to fall on him. Then he realizes it's the hand of Princess Toadstool, reaching down to lift him into Yoshi's mouth.

SWOOSH!

The princess grabs him by his red overalls and lifts him through the air. To the tiny Mario, it seems as if he's soaring a hundred miles above the ground. Suddenly he's hanging upside-down above a giant, dark cavern lined with rows of sharp white rocks.

"That's no cavern," he says. "That's Yoshi's mouth! Maybe this wasn't such a good idea. Hey!" he shouts. "Put me down!"

The princess hears Mario squeaking.

"He's so brave," she says to Toad and the King, wiping a tear from her eye. Then she lets go of Mario's overalls.

"Watch out below!" Mario yells as he plunges down.

**What will happen to Mario next?
It's up to you to make the choices that will get safely through this indigestible adventure!**

Nintendo® Adventure Books Available in Mammoth:

DOUBLE TROUBLE ✓
LEAPING LIZARDS ✓
MONSTER MIX-UP ✓
KOOPA CAPERS
PIPE DOWN!
DOORS TO DOOM
DINOSAUR DILEMMA
FLOWN THE KOOPA
THE CRYSTAL TRAP ✓
THE SHADOW PRINCE ✓
UNJUST DESSERTS ✓
BRAIN DRAIN

Nintendo Adventure Books

FEATURING THE SUPER MARIO BROS.®

11
UNJUST DESSERTS
By Matt Wayne

MAMMOTH

This book is dedicated to Fran, Paul and Viola

This book is a work of fiction. Names, characters, places and incidents are either the product of the author's imagination or are used fictitiously. Any resemblance to actual events or locales or persons, living or dead, is entirely coincidental.

First published in the USA 1992 by Pocket Books,
a division of Simon & Schuster
First published in Great Britain 1993 by Mammoth
an imprint of Reed Consumer Books Ltd
Michelin House, 81 Fulham Road, London SW3 6RB
and Auckland, Melbourne, Singapore and Toronto

Copyright © 1992 by Nintendo. All Rights Reserved.
Cover artwork copyright © 1992 Nintendo

Nintendo, Super Mario Bros. and Yoshi, Mario, Luigi, Bowser the Koopa King and Toad are trademarks of Nintendo.

ISBN 0 7497 1546 4

A CIP catalogue record for this title
is available from the British Library

Printed and bound in Great Britain
by Cox & Wyman Ltd, Reading, Berkshire

This paperback is sold subject to the condition
that it shall not, by way of trade or otherwise,
be lent, resold, hired out, or otherwise circulated
without the publisher's prior consent in any form
of binding or cover other than that in which
it is published and without a similar condition
including this condition being imposed
on the subsequent purchaser.

Creative Media Applications, Inc.
Series developed by Dan Oehlsen, Lary Rosenblatt &
Barbara Stewart
Art direction by Fabia Wargin Design
Cover painting by Greg Wray
Puzzle art by Josie Koehne
Edited by Eloise Flood
Special thanks to Ruth Ashby, Lisa Clancy, Paolo Pepe &
George Sinfield

Dear Game Player:

You are about to guide me through a great adventure. As you read this book, you will help me decide where to go and what to do. Whether I succeed or fail is up to you.

At the end of every chapter, you will make choices that determine what happens next. Special puzzles will help you decide what I should do—if you can solve them. The chapters in this book are in a special order. Sometimes you must go backward in order to go forward, if you know what I mean.

Along the way, you'll find many different items to help me with my quest. When you read that I have found something, such as the medicine bottle, you'll see a box like the one below:

> *****Mario now has the medicine bottle.*****
> **Turn to page 12.**

Use page 121 to keep track of the things you collect and to keep score.

Good luck!
Driplessly yours,

Mario

1

"Happy birthday, Yoshi!"

The King of the Mushrooms is throwing a birthday party for his favorite dinosaur, Yoshi, and everyone is invited—including those two famous plumbers, Mario and Luigi. Practically the entire Mushroom Kingdom is squeezed into the great hall of the palace.

Gulp! "Great party, huh, Mario?" says Mario's younger brother Luigi through bites of pizza. The tall, skinny plumber has one slice in each hand and a third balanced on top of his green plumber's cap.

"You think you have enough?" asks Mario.

A worried look crosses Luigi's face. "Maybe not," he answers and runs back to the food tables, bobbing through the packed crowd of mushrooms.

A hush falls as the Mushroom King gets up to speak. "By royal proclamation, I declare this to be Yoshi Day!" he says.

1

"Yay!" Everyone starts to cheer and applaud. "Speech! Speech!" they cry.

The bright green dinosaur lumbers up to the front of the room. "Plorp!" he says.

"Yay!" everyone cheers again.

"Not much of a speech," Mario says to Princess Toadstool, daughter of the king.

"What do you expect?" she replies. "Yoshi's just a baby. Give him a few years."

"Some baby," says Mario, looking at the six-foot tall dinosaur.

Toad, the royal mushroom retainer, wheels out a mammoth birthday cake. It's covered with thick orange and green icing and dotted with candied meatballs. At the very top, surrounded by candles, is a purple cherry the size of a grapefruit.

"Make a wish!" cries the princess. Yoshi closes his eyes and blows out the candles, splattering dozens of mushrooms with icing.

Mario ducks, as the icing goes flying, and spots some coins on the floor. "Hmm," he says, picking them up. "Party favors!"

Meanwhile, Yoshi grabs the giant purple cherry from the top of the cake and gulps it down in one bite.

"Mario, something's wrong with Yoshi!" cries Princess Toadstool a second later.

"What is it?" asks Mario.

"He's turning purple, for one thing," answers the princess.

"Now that you mention it, he does look a little strange," says Mario. They rush to Yoshi, who's rubbing his belly with one hand and patting his head with the other.

"Wow, look at that!" says Mario.

"I told you, he's sick!" says the princess.

"No, I mean he can rub his belly and pat his head at the same time," says Mario. "That's pretty neat!"

"Mario!" the princess says impatiently. "Yoshi, do you have a stomach-ache?" she asks the dinosaur.

Yoshi nods his head sadly and starts to turn orange. Then his eyes light up and he reaches for his birthday cake.

"He wants to eat the cake," Mario says. "Maybe it will settle his stomach."

"Or maybe it'll make him sicker," says Princess Toadstool. "Don't let him eat!"

Solve this puzzle to help decide what Mario should do:

- Pick one of the spaghetti strands by Mario's feet and follow it to the end. Then follow the advice written on the cake there.

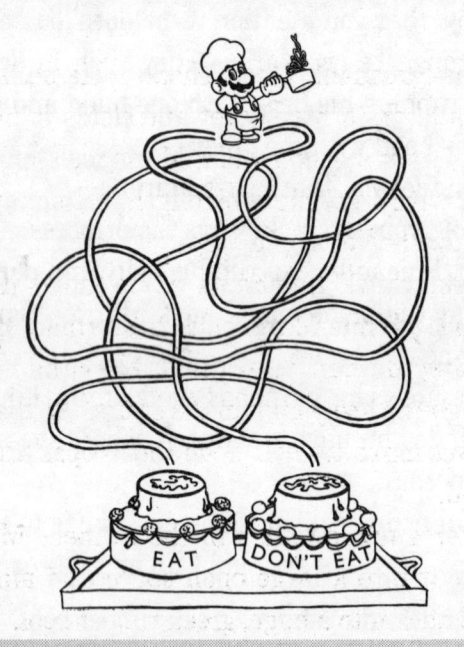

Mario collects 10 coins.

If you reached the cake that says EAT, turn to page 32.

If you reached the cake that says DON'T EAT, turn to page 106.

2

"The Starman!" Mario shouts. He pulls the blue star from his pocket and holds it in his hand. As it starts to glow, Mario feels himself filled with invincible strength. He charges right for the horde of Koopas.

"Take that!" he shouts as he mows down enemies. While Mario holds a Starman, nothing they do can stop him. He runs right through the army and up the stairs. At the top he dives into a tunnel. Soon the Koopas are far behind.

After a few minutes in the tunnel, Mario pops out into a large open space and almost flies smack into a huge, green rubber boot.

"Luigi!" Mario shouts at the sight of his brother's right toe.

"About time," Luigi mutters.

Turn to page 6.

3

Mario runs over and hugs the toe of the rubber boot. "Little brother, I've found you!" he cries happily.

"Who are you calling little?" replies Luigi in a huge, booming voice.

Mario looks up, but Luigi's face is too far above him to see clearly.

"Don't worry, Luigi," Mario says. "I'm here to rescue you."

"Oh, yeah?" Luigi says sourly. "You've been saying that all day. Exactly how do you plan to get me out?"

> ***** Mario gets 100 points for reaching Luigi.*****
>
> **If Mario has the medicine bottle, turn to page 62.**
>
> **If Mario doesn't have the medicine bottle, turn to page 72.**

4

CRASH!

Yoshi lands with a thud. So does Mario.

"I guess the blue-shell spell has worn off," he says as he gets up and dusts himself off. "Where am I now?"

By the light of his headlamp, Mario sees that he's in the middle of a large green chamber full of pits and waterfalls.

RUMBLE! RUMBLE!

"Sounds like Yoshi has indigestion," Mario says. "That'll happen when you go around swallowing plumbers."

RUMBLE! RUMBLE!

"Funny," Mario says, "but it sounds almost like a herd of . . . Dino-Rhinos?!"

Mario turns just in time to see a whole herd of Dino-Rhinos come rumbling around a brown hill. Their short, blunt horns are lowered and they charge right at him.

"Uh-oh!" he gulps and jumps out of the way

of the first rhino. He does a somersault over the second, then leaps on tip-toe over a third. The charging, snorting rhinos are too slow and clumsy to catch him and soon he's jumped over all of them.

"Phew," he sighs with relief. "Time to get out of here."

Mario hops along a stream of brown, bubbling liquid. Soon he reaches a vast lake of the stuff. Mario can't see any way around.

"Do I have to swim?" he wonders. He sniffs the bubbling lake. "Hmmm, this is Koopa Kola. You're not supposed to swim in Koopa Kola. Or maybe you're not supposed to swim in Green Fizz? Or maybe it's Boomer Berry juice? I just saw an article about this in the *Mushroom Kingdom Health News*."

Solve this puzzle to find out which of the three liquids is the one that Mario shouldn't swim in.

• Here's a picture from the *Mushroom Kingdom Health News*. One glass holds Koopa Kola, one holds Boomer Berry juice and one holds Green Fizz. You can't see how much each glass holds, but luckily the editors included this information:

- There's exactly 22 ounces of the drink that you should never swim in.
- There's one quart plus one ounce of Boomer Berry juice.
- There's twice as much Koopa Kola as Green Fizz.
- There's exactly as much Boomer Berry juice as the Green Fizz and Koopa Kola added together.
- Which is the drink that Mario shouldn't swim in?

If you think Mario should swim, turn to page 35.

If you don't think he should swim, turn to page 13.

5

The dino doctor remembers suddenly. "Of course, Luigi has to take the medicine! It will shrink him and then he can just crawl out of Yoshi. Good thing we didn't give it to Yoshi—he would have shrunk with Luigi still inside him."

"Great!" says Mario. "Only, how are we supposed to get it to Luigi? Mail it to him?"

"No, the Royal Post Office is too slow," says the king.

"Don't worry," answers Doc Drake. He reaches into his bag again and comes up with a ball of string. "We'll just lower it to him on this string."

Quickly, the dino doctor ties the end of the string around the small bottle.

"Now, hold still, Yoshi, and open wide," he says as he walks up to the large dinosaur.

"Florp!" says Yoshi.

"I think that means okay," says the princess.

"Unless it means, 'I feel like swallowing a dino doctor,'" says Toad.

But Yoshi doesn't try to swallow Doc Drake. He opens his mouth very wide and allows the dino doctor to lower the bottle down his throat.

"Yurmf!!" cries Luigi from inside Yoshi.

"I think it hit him on the head," says Mario. "Luigi!" he calls. "The bottle! Drink it!"

Yoshi looks at Mario, then grins, closes his mouth, and swallows. The string disappears into his mouth.

Gulp!

"No!" shouts Mario. "Not you, Yoshi! Doc, he swallowed the string!"

"I know," says the duck, rubbing his wrist. "He almost took my hand with it!"

Mario gets 50 points for guessing that Luigi is the one who's supposed to take the medicine.

Turn to page 79.

6

"This is ridiculous!" Mario says, going through the pockets of his overalls again. "A plumber without a wrench! I'm a disgrace to my profession! How will I be able to face the guys back at the Plunger's Lodge?

"My reputation is ruined," he groans sadly. "Not only that, I have to go back over the Wigglers, the Koopa Troopas and the Sumo Brothers. It'll take me forever to reach Luigi now. Oh well, maybe someone else will rescue him—someday."

GAME OVER!

7

"I can't swim in this," says Mario, as he touches the Koopa Kola with his toe.

"You're right," says a high, squeaky voice. The rounded blue head of a dolphin pokes up from the lake of Koopa Kola.

"A dolphin?" Mario says in surprise. "How did you get here?"

"I'm a micro-dolphin," the animal answers. "Name's Donny. I live here. But how did you get here? Did somebody call for a plumber?"

"No," Mario says. "But this place could use one." He tells the micro-dolphin the story of how Luigi got swallowed by Yoshi.

"Yoshi?" Donny says. "Who's Yoshi?"

"Why, Yoshi's the dinosaur you live in," Mario answers, surprised.

Donny lets out a loud, buzzing laugh. "Dinosaur? Hear that, guys?" he yells. "This plumber says we live inside a dinosaur."

Four more dolphin heads break the surface of the Kola lake. They laugh loudly.

"But you do," Mario insists.

"Very funny," Donny replies. "Next you'll be telling us the world is round."

Mario shrugs. "Forget it," he says.

"Anyway, it's a good thing you didn't try to swim through this stuff," Donny says. "Kola is too sticky for you to get through without flippers. Come on, guys, let's give the little plumber a hand. Jump on board!"

"Okay. Thanks," says Mario, and he steps on Donny's back.

Solve this puzzle to score extra points:

• There are many ways across the sea of Koopa Kola, if you use the dolphins to help you. Get Mario through the maze. Every time you pass over a dolphin Mario gets 2 coins.

Turn to page 119.

8

"I could use a Starman right now," Mario says as he runs back down the stairs. "I wonder if there are any that I missed on my way. Too late to look now."

As he runs down the stairs he slips and falls into the lake of Koopa Kola. Quickly, he becomes stuck in the gooey brown liquid.

"Oh, no!" he moans. "I'm a sitting duck for those Koopas. I'll never get out of here. Someone else will have to rescue Luigi—and me, too, come to think of it."

GAME OVER!

9

"My flying suit," Mario cries. "Good thing I brought it!"

He quickly slips on his suit and flies off to the magic daisies. As soon as he lands he takes a bite from one of the petals.

"Mmm," he says. "This is better than anything Luigi had to eat today!"

Whoosh!

Suddenly, the tiny plumber is tiny no longer. He pops up in the middle of Luigi, the princess and the rest of his friends.

"Mario!" cries the princess. "How did you get here?"

"You could say I ate right," he answers.

Mario gains 200 points for getting back to normal size.

Turn to page 100.

10

"That fungus looks like it's alive," Mario says. "I'm going to stay on the brown spots."

Carefully Mario steps onto the nearest brown spot. Nothing happens.

"I guess I was right," he sighs and starts jumping from spot to spot.

"HOO, HOO!"

Mario's ears are blasted by loud laughter. The whole cavern starts to shake.

"What's happening?" Mario shouts, leaping to the next spot.

"HAW, HAW, HAW!"

Suddenly the whole cavern tilts sideways and Mario starts rolling downhill, bouncing over fungus and brown patches.

"Yoshi's laughing!" he says as he rolls. "Those brown patches are his ticklish spots! How dumb can you get! Everyone knows a dinosaur is most ticklish on his back!"

Slipping and sliding, Mario rolls right into a large pipe opening at the end of the cavern.

"Well, at least I got where I wanted to go," he says, and starts crawling through the pipe.

Turn to page 92.

11

"They all look the same to me," says Mario. Shrugging his shoulders, he plunges into the left-hand tunnel. The beam from his plumber's cap shines on rounded yellow walls.

"Looks like a pipe I was in last week," he says as he slogs through the grape punch. Ahead of him, the passageway is blocked by a large, round, red-and-brown boulder.

"What is that?" Mario wonders. He pushes the boulder with his finger and a hunk of it comes away. Mario sniffs the brown stuff.

"It's a meatball!" he says. "I've got to remind Yoshi to chew his food before he swallows!" With a few kicks of his boots, Mario breaks the meatball into pieces. It floats away on the grape punch.

Just beyond, the pipe empties out into another chamber. The walls are green and spotted with large lumps.

"Dinosaurs sure are weird inside," Mario says to himself.

Bizzup! Breezoop!

"What's that?" Mario cries, just as a swarm of flat bug-like creatures comes crawling up out of a hole in the floor. Each is about as big as Mario's foot, with six long arms and two big crab-like claws. As Mario watches, the bugs grab pieces of meatball and bits of spaghetti floating in the punch and throw them down the hole.

"I guess they work here," Mario says.

Clank! Buzz!

A harsh, rasping noise like a buzzsaw comes from the hole in the floor. Then three of the shiny orange bugs grab Mario and start hauling him toward the hole.

"Hey, I'm no meatball!" Mario shouts. He shakes himself loose. Then he feels himself being pulled in another direction. He looks down and sees a bunch of round, blue bugs pulling him toward a different hole—this one is in the wall.

Gurgle! Glug!

Mario hears loud, wet sucking noises coming from inside the hole in the wall.

"Yuck!" he says, shaking free of the blue bugs. "I'm not going in there!"

Mario sees a bunch of the orange bugs heading for him again. He jumps up and lands on the back of one of them.

SQUOOSH!

It disappears under the grape punch. He jumps again, and lands on a blue bug.

SQUISH!

Using the bugs as stepping stones, he quickly bounces around the room, looking for another way out, but there isn't any.

"Well, here's a problem," Mario says. "Both ways out of here are totally gross. But I have to choose one."

Solve this puzzle to see which way Mario goes:

• Get Mario to the other side of the room by jumping from bug to bug. Add or subtract the number of points on each. Mario can move in any direction, but he can't jump on the same bug twice.

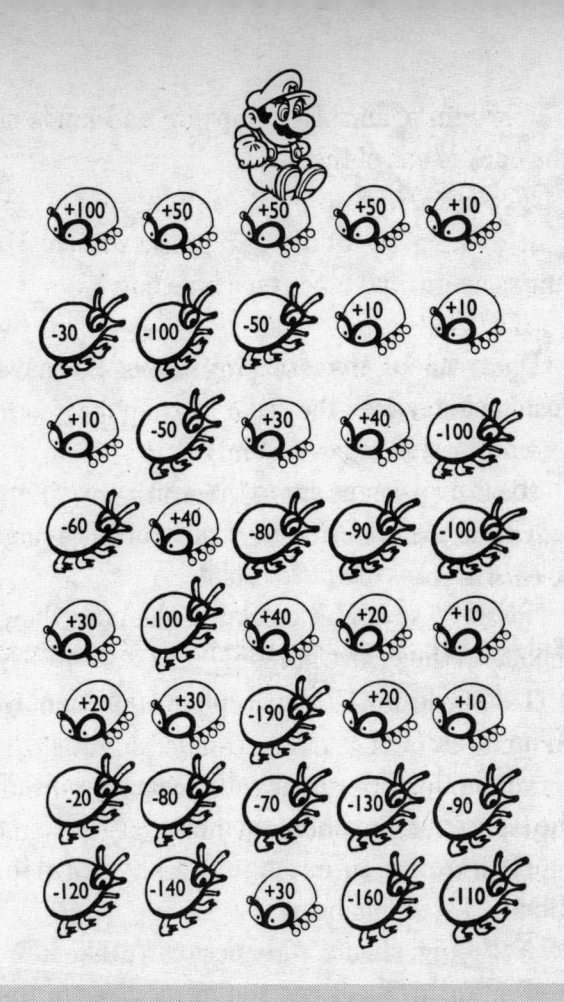

Add Mario's score to his total.

If Mario scored less than 300, turn to page 90.

If Mario scored more than 300,
turn to page 116.

12

"Sorry about that," Mario replies. "What's Yoshi doing now?"

"Shh!" says Luigi. "Listen!"

Mario presses his ear to the wall.

"Good, Yoshi," Princess Toadstool is saying. "Play with the cute little rabbit."

"Rabbit?" says Mario. "Since when are there rabbits in the palace garden?"

"I don't know," Luigi replies impatiently. "Who cares?"

"Oh, is the nice rabbit eating gonzo grapes?" the princess says at that moment.

"He's going to eat again," says Mario. "Should I start bouncing?"

"No!" Luigi shouts. "My nose can't take it."

"No, Yoshi, don't eat the grapes," says the princess.

"Oh, no!" shouts Luigi. "The grapes are landing on my head! Yeow!"

"Don't be such a big baby," Mario tells him. "They're only grapes!"

"They're not grapes!" Luigi shouts. "They're tiny Koopa Troopas! Ouch!"

"Hey, that's no rabbit!" Mario hears Princess Toadstool yell. "It's Magikoopa!"

"Mario!" Luigi shouts. "Magikoopa shrank Bowser's whole army and disguised them as gonzo grapes. There's a mecha-Koopa! And some mini-Ninjis! Ouch! Mario, help me!"

"Don't worry!" Mario shouts at Luigi's nose through the chamber wall. "I'm coming!"

Mario slides down the wall and quickly finds a tunnel that seems to lead to Luigi.

"I'm coming!" he shouts again.

"No you're not!" someone answers.

The light from his cap shines into the tunnel and shows Mario two of Bowser's Sumo Brothers waddling straight at him.

Mario loses 100 points for letting Yoshi eat the grapes.

Turn to page 57.

13

"There he is!" shouts a tiny Bowser Koopa. "Charge!"

While Princess Toadstool and Luigi are arguing with Doc Drake, Mario sees all of Bowser's shrunken army come charging at him from behind a pebble. Dino-Rhinos, Wigglers, mini-Ninjis, Shyguys and a whole battalion of Koopa Troopas run toward him.

"I forgot about those creeps," Mario sighs. "They all got out of Yoshi, too."

Then Mario is dodging Koopa shells, jumping over Shyguys and squashing Wigglers.

"Phew," he grunts as he leaps over twenty screaming mini-Ninjis. "This is a lot of meanies, even for a super plumber like me. I could use some help."

If Mario has the flower, turn to page 96.

If Mario does not have the flower turn to page 86.

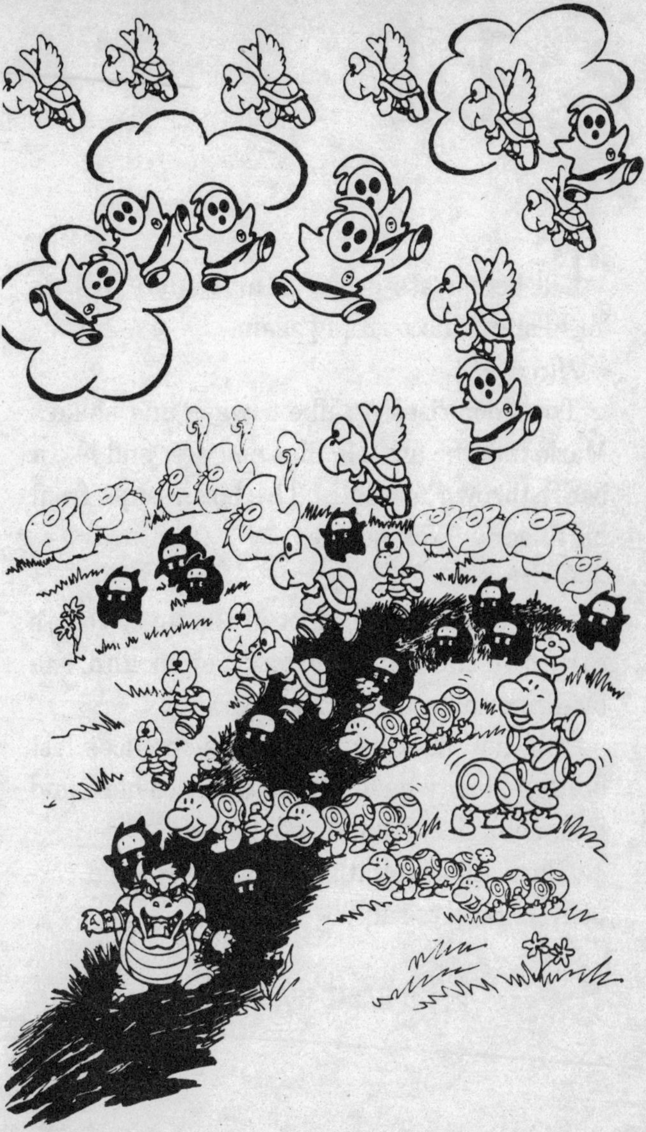

14

"I'd better stay put," Mario says, just as Yoshi starts hiccoughing again.

Hiccough!

The floor rises up like a wave and shakes Mario into the air. He flips end over end like a badly-thrown football. The bottle slips from his fingers. "No!" he cries.

Crash!

Mario lands softly, right in the tip of Yoshi's tail, but the bottle breaks open and the medicine spills all over the floor.

"Oh, no!" he says. "That was the doc's last bottle. Now I have to climb out of here and find a new one. That'll take forever!"

"Plus, it shrank all this perfectly good carpeting," he says sadly.

GAME OVER!

15

"Luigi, talk to me!" Mario shouts at Yoshi's belly. "Are you all right?"

"Mmf! Hmmmf!" comes the muffled reply from inside Yoshi.

"What's he saying?" asks Toad, still wiping bits of cake off his polka-dot cap.

"I think he's saying *'Mmf! Hmmmf!'*" says the king helpfully.

"Come over by his head," says Princess Toadstool, pointing to a bump by Yoshi's belly button. "You can hear him better."

"That's not his head," says Mario. He points to a large lump on Yoshi's side. "This is!"

"No," says Toad, pointing in another direction. "It's over here."

"Mmf! Hmmmf!" Luigi shouts again.

"I'm not sure, but I think he's saying 'Get me out of here,'" says Toad.

"Only one person can help," says the princess. "Doc Drake, the dino doctor."

29

"Not him!" calls a voice. "I wouldn't trust him one bit."

Out of the crowd steps a short, round mushroom Mario has never seen before.

"My name is Fungus Cap," he says. "And I say Doc Drake is a quack."

"Of course he's a quack," answers the princess. "After all, he's a giant mallard. But he's the best dino doctor in the Mushroom Kingdom."

"My cousin's dino had the same problem," says Fungus Cap. "I just gave him one of these." He pulls out a large bottle filled with pink pills. "Let me give one to Yoshi."

"I don't know," says Mario. "Are you sure those things work?"

Solve this puzzle to help Mario decide what to do:

- On the next page is a picture of Doc Drake's office. In it are some clues about whether he is a good dino doctor. Read the rules and look at the picture to decide if Mario should let the doctor treat Yoshi.

1. Good dino doctors never have less than 5 things on their desks.

2. All good dino doctors have the same number of diplomas on their wall.

3. If a bad dino doctor has an even number of things on his desk, he has more diplomas on his wall than a good dino doctor.

4. A good dino doctor always has half as many diplomas on his wall as things on his desk.

> **If you think Mario should call the Dino Doctor, turn to page 110.**
>
> **If you think Mario should listen to Fungus Cap, turn to page 88.**

16

Yoshi grabs a hunk of cake and stuffs it into his mouth. The dinosaur turns pale.

Rumble! Rumble!

"What's that noise?" asks Toad.

"It's an earthquake!" yells the king.

"No!" shouts the princess. "It's Yoshi's stomach! He's going to explode!"

"Worse," says Mario. "He's going to belch!"

Boof!

"Pee-yew!" says Mario holding his nose. "What a smell!"

Panicked mushrooms run for the exits. One bumps into Mario. Five coins spill out of the plumber's pocket and roll away.

"Watch out!" shouts Princess Toadstool. "He's going to eat again. Mario, stop him!"

Mario loses 5 coins.
Turn to page 106.

17

Mario hops over to Luigi's green rubber boot. With a mighty leap, he gets on top.

"I don't know why you're so worried," Luigi says to the princess at that moment. "Mario's smart enough to stay away from our feet."

"Maybe I'm even smarter than that," Mario says, and he takes out the fireflower.

Whoosh!

With a shower of orange sparks, Mario sends a tiny fireball crashing into the right side of Luigi's foot.

"YEOW!" Luigi yells and jumps to his left, almost halfway to the daisies.

"Luigi! Stand still!" shouts Princess Toadstool.

"Something bit me!" Luigi complains.

"Here's another bite," says Mario and he sends another fireball into Luigi's foot.

"YEOW!" Luigi jumps again.

"Luigi!" says the princess.

"I can't help it," he says.

"Almost there," says Mario. "Just a little more to the right."

"YIKES!" shouts Luigi.

"Thanks, little brother," cries Mario as he slides off and runs to the daisies. With a leap, he reaches one of the white petals and takes a bite.

Swoosh!

Mario zooms back up to his regular size.

"Mario!" shouts Princess Toadstool. "Where'd you come from?"

"Oh, someone gave me a lift," he answers.

Mario gets 200 points for getting back to normal size.

Turn to page 100.

18

"What harm can a little swimming do?" Mario says to himself, and dives into the lake. He takes a few strokes. Then he notices that the Kola is forming little brown crystals on his plumber's overalls.

"Yuck!" he says.

Soon his whole body is coated with thick, brown, Kola sludge. He can barely move his arms and legs.

"Now I remember!" he moans. "You're not supposed to swim in Koopa Kola, because it will stick all over you!"

By this time, it's all Mario can do just to flip over onto his back, where he floats helplessly.

"Oh, no!" he sighs. "I'm stuck here until all this Kola dries up. Poor Luigi!"

GAME OVER!

19

"Mario?" Luigi booms.

Mario gazes around. He's in pitch darkness, somewhere inside his brother.

"Drat!" he says. "The light on my cap is off." He reaches up and gives it a whack with one hand.

"Ouch! My head!" he says as the light comes on. "Hmm. From the looks of this place I must be in Luigi's stomach. Yuck!"

"Mario, where are you?" calls Luigi.

"I'm in here!" Mario shouts back. "You swallowed me by mistake!"

That's what Mario says. But what Luigi hears is: "MM MEM SWAB MUB BUB!"

"Hey, the rumbling in my stomach sounds a little like Mario," says Luigi. "I must be really hungry."

"Hungry!" Mario shouts. "I'll show you hungry!" And he kicks the wall of Luigi's stomach with his boot.

"Yeow!" Luigi shouts. "That's Mario, all right. Golly, I must've swallowed him by mistake. I'd better look for that bottle."

"Bottle?" Mario says. "Oh, no! If he drinks the medicine now, he'll shrink with me inside him. Luigi! Don't do it!"

"Hey, Mario, I think I found it!" Luigi shouts.

Thud! Something large and heavy lands on Mario's head. He sprawls on the floor.

"Thanks for cushioning my fall," says a nasty turtlish voice.

Mario turns and looks right into the warty face of Bowser Koopa!

"Luigi swallowed you?" Mario says. "This is crazy."

"What do you expect?" sneers Bowser. "He's your brother."

"Hey, nobody insults my brother," Mario says, pushing Bowser aside and standing up. "Except me, that is!"

"Have some pizza," says Bowser with a wicked laugh. He grabs a chunk of pizza as big as a ping pong table and hurls it at Mario. It covers him like a gooey cheese blanket.

"That's it!" Mario shouts, wiping tomato sauce from his face. He grabs a giant ravioli and throws it like a saucer at Bowser's head.

Splat! The ravioli bursts, showering them both with bits of pasta and meat.

"What's going on in there?" Luigi calls, holding his stomach. "I just heard Doc Drake outside. He says he remembered another way to get me out. He's going to feed Yoshi a plant called the threelip. He thinks that'll make Yoshi spit me out."

Mario stops fighting. Bowser hits him in the face with a humongous lasagna noodle.

"He thinks?" Mario says. "Oh, no! That Doc Drake makes me nervous. Maybe I should try to stop him. But how?"

Solve this puzzle to see if Yoshi should eat the threelip.

- Mario is sorting flowers into two piles. One pile contains flowers that Yoshi should not eat. The other pile contains flowers that Yoshi should eat. Mario is holding the threelip. Which pile should it go in? (Hint: Look at the relationship between the leaves and pedals on each flower.)

Don't Eat **Eat**

If you think Yoshi should eat the threelip, turn to page 103.

If you think Yoshi shouldn't eat the threelip, turn to page 56.

20

"Now I remember," Mario says. "Dinos are ticklish on their backs. I bet those brown patches are Yoshi's ticklish spots. I'm going to stay on the fungus."

Carefully he steps onto the nearest green spot. He sinks up to his ankles in the soft squishy muck.

Squoosh!

Suddenly the fungus spot comes alive—a stringy, sticky net of gunk grows up right in front of Mario. Luckily, the tiny plumber can easily dodge it, hopping to the next spot.

Squoosh! Squash!

"A Super Mario is smarter than a fungus any day!" Mario cries proudly, and he begins bouncing from spot to spot, using the green fungus nets as trampolines. In no time at all he's bounced clear across the cavern.

"Take that, you funguses!" he shouts. "Or is that fungi?"

He's about to crawl into a large pipe when he sees a shimmering blue Starman lying on the ground.

"How'd that get here?" he wonders. "Well, wherever it came from, a Starman always comes in handy." He picks up the strange, glowing blue star and puts it in a pocket of his overalls. Then he ducks into the pipe and starts crawling.

Mario now has the Starman.

Mario gets 100 points for getting through the fungus.

Turn to page 92.

21

BLAM! Mario smashes the blue shell and it explodes in a shower of sparks. Suddenly, the tunnel starts to glow with blue light.

"What's happening?" says one of the Sumo Brothers who wakes up at that moment. "Why does it feel like we're in an elevator?"

"You're dreaming," says the other Sumo Brother. "Go back to sleep."

"He's not dreaming," Mario says. "Yoshi is flying! That's what the blue shells make him do. They make him fly!"

"So big deal," snorts the first Sumo. "He goes up like a birdy."

"Yes," says Mario, looking for a hand-hold. "But what goes up must come down!"

As he says it, the floor falls out from underneath them!

"He's diving!" Mario shouts as he, the Sumo Brothers and the Koopa Troopas float above the floor.

"Look, we're weightless!" shouts one of the Sumo Brothers.

"Good," says the other. "Now I don't have to go on that diet."

With a thud, they fall to the ground as Yoshi starts soaring up again.

"Hey, this is fun," says one of the Sumos. "Almost as much fun as smashing plumbers. Which reminds me!"

The Sumo Brothers get set to charge Mario again, but as they do, Yoshi decides to do a loop-the-loop. Everything in the tunnel turns upside down.

"Yeow!" shout the Sumo Brothers as they slide down a pipe opening in the ceiling.

"Bye-bye, bozos!" Mario laughs. "That's pretty funny. Heh, heh . . . yeeooow!"

Wwoosh!

Mario slides into a pipe in the tunnel wall as Yoshi turns over again.

"This dinosaur needs seatbelts!" Mario grumbles as he falls through the darkness.

Turn to page 7.

22

"Wow!" Mario says. "This bottle is going to be hard to carry. I'd better wait here until the hiccoughing stops."

HICCOUGH!

Yoshi's tail flies up and then smacks down to the ground, with Mario inside it.

"Yikes!" he mutters. "That was close. I almost dropped the bottle."

"Wewark! Klooper!" Luigi's voice sounds as if it's miles away.

"What's he saying?" Mario wonders. "He sounds scared or angry or something."

Mario tries to pull on his mustache without letting go of the bottle. "On second thought," he thinks, "Maybe I should get back to Luigi as fast as I can. No telling what might happen inside this dino."

Solve this puzzle to figure out what Mario should do:

- Look at the pictures of Bowser Koopa. How many are exactly the same?

If you think an even number are the same, turn to page 28.

If you think an odd number are the same, turn to page 117.

45

23

"I remember," says the dino doctor. "Give the medicine to Yoshi." He empties the bottle into Yoshi's very large mouth.

"You know, the room seems to be getting larger," says Toad as they all watch Yoshi.

"Wait a minute!" shouts the princess. "The room isn't getting larger! Yoshi's getting smaller!"

She's right! Yoshi is shrinking before their very eyes.

"Oh, no!" cries Doc Drake. "I've made a terrible mistake! That's shrinking medicine and I should have given it to Luigi!"

Soon Yoshi is only two feet tall . . . and still shrinking.

"What are we going to do?" wails Mario. "We'll never get Luigi out now!"

GAME OVER!

24

"Daisies?" Mario repeats, overhearing Doc Drake's explanation. "How am I supposed to get over there? It's too far to fly, even with a flying suit."

BOOM! BOOM!

The ground starts to shake and Mario falls down.

"What's happening now?" he yells.

"Yoshi!" Princess Toadstool shouts. "Stand still. You might step on Mario!"

Mario looks up and sees Yoshi's foot close by like a huge green, scaly mountain.

BOOM!

Something else shakes the ground.

"Luigi!" the Princess shouts. "That goes for you, too."

"Sorry," says Luigi. "My foot fell asleep."

Mario sees Luigi's green rubber boot rising up out of the grass nearby.

"Hmm," Mario thinks. "Either of those two could get me to the daisies. I'll just climb on one of their feet. The only problem is, which one?"

Solve this puzzle to find out who can get Mario to the daisies.

• Get Luigi or Yoshi across by hopping from mushroom to mushroom until they reach the last row. Each of them has to follow a different rule. Luigi can only jump onto a mushroom with the same or fewer spots than the one he's on. Yoshi can only jump onto a mushroom with the same or more spots than the one he's on. Only one can get across. Who is it?

If you think Mario should go with Luigi, turn to page 33.

If you think Mario should go with Yoshi, turn to page 60.

25

Mario jumps over the last of the Koopa Troopas and ducks into a large pipe.

"Wigglers!" he cries. "I hate those creepy things!"

A horde of catepillar-like monsters are inching their way down the tunnel, making disgusting munching noises as they go.

"On the bright side, I never met a Wiggler I couldn't jump over," Mario says. He bounces over the Wigglers and keeps running down the tunnel. But in a minute he has to screech to a halt again, as the tunnel ends at a large round valve.

Mario turns just in time to see the Wigglers coming back toward him.

"No fair," he says. "They don't even have to turn around, they just back up. I'll just open this valve and keep going."

He grabs the nut that holds the valve closed and tries to twist it open.

"Ugh!" he grunts. "It's stuck. What I need is a good wrench!"

If Mario has the wrench, turn to page 61.

If Mario doesn't have the wrench, turn to page 12.

26

BLAM! Mario smashes the yellow shell. It explodes in a shower of sparks. Suddenly the tunnel starts glowing with yellow light.

"Yoshi's changing!" Mario thinks and quickly grabs hold of the wall.

BOOM! BOOM!

It's like an earthquake inside Yoshi. Everybody is thrown through the air as the dino starts stamping the ground. Goombas fly from side to side, bouncing off the walls. Koopa Troopas bang into the ceiling. Mario holds on to the wall with all his strength.

Finally the shaking stops. Mario is still standing, but Koopa commandos are sprawled on the floor.

"Thanks, guys!" Mario shouts as he leaps from Troopa to Troopa. "But you shouldn't be lying down on the job!"

Solve this puzzle to score extra points:

- As Mario goes on his way toward Luigi, he

collects as many coins as there are plates on the backs of the Koopa Troopas he jumps on. He can start anywhere on the top row and leap from Troopa to Troopa in any direction. He may only move to a Troopa with the same or a greater number of plates on his shell, and he can't land on the same Troopa twice. Add up the plates on the backs of the Troopas Mario lands on and add the total to your score.

Turn to page 50.

27

"Luigi, be a man," Mario advises. "A little smell won't hurt you."

"I can't take it!" wails Luigi.

"Well, I—" Mario begins.

"Too late," Luigi cries. "Oh, no!"

"Don't yell so much," Mario calls to his brother. "You'll give Yoshi the—"

HICCOUGH!

The force of Yoshi's hiccough throws Mario across the chamber and he falls into a dark tunnel. He bounces downward for a long time, then rolls gently onto a soft floor covered with long, green hair.

"Hmm," Mario says. "I always wanted a carpet like this for our plumber's shop. I'll have to ask Yoshi where he got it."

He looks around and sees that the tunnel narrows and then ends a little ways ahead. "Wow!" he says, catching his breath. "I must have fallen all the way into Yoshi's tail."

HICCOUGH!

Yoshi hiccoughs again and his tail swings wildly from side to side. While Mario holds on, something large and hard bonks him right in the head.

"Ouch!" he says. He turns his light around. There in the beam is a large brown bottle, almost as tall as he is.

"Eureka!" Mario yells. "The shrink medicine!"

He grabs the bottle and hugs it with one arm just as Yoshi starts hiccoughing again.

Mario now has the medicine bottle.
Turn to page 44.

28

"I don't trust that duck's memory," Mario says. He kicks Luigi's stomach.

"Oof!" grunts Luigi, holding his stomach. "Okay, okay, I get the hint." Luigi kicks Yoshi.

"GORF!" shouts Yoshi, and he starts running away from Doc Drake, with Luigi bouncing along inside him.

Inside Luigi, Mario turns to face Bowser. But the Koopa king has vanished!

"So long, sucker!" Bowser's voice floats from somewhere above him. "The threelip was your only chance to get out of here! It only grows every two years and has to be eaten fresh! Luckily, I have my own way of getting out. See you in a couple of years!"

"Two years," Mario groans. "I can't take it!"

GAME OVER!

29

"Okay, you Sumos," Mario grumbles as he dusts himself off. "I've had enough of this."

"Oh, yeah?" sneers one of the Sumos. He turns to the other rotund wrestler. "Let's knock this plumber down the drain!"

The two Sumo Brothers stand on opposite sides of Mario and dig in their heels, then they both charge. But Mario leaps lightly into the air and the two Sumos run head first—right into each other!

KA-BLAM!

"I guess I threw a wrench into your plans," Mario says as the two Sumos sprawl face down on the floor.

CRACK!

Mario ducks as he hears the sound of a Koopa shell being fired.

"Uh-oh. Here comes the rest of Bowser's army," he says.

Coming down the tunnel is a squad of Koopa

Troopas. Mario can see the cannons on the turtles' backs, firing blue and yellow Koopa shells.

A yellow shell comes zooming at Mario and he ducks. Then a Koopa Troopa launches a blue shell. Mario dodges that one also.

"Think fast," Mario says to himself. "If I smash a yellow shell, it will make Yoshi's insides shake. But I can't remember what the blue shells do."

Just then a blue and a yellow shell come flying right for Mario.

"What'll I do now?" he wonders.

Solve this puzzle to find out what the blue shells do to Yoshi.

- Look at the list of Koopa commandos, find the names in the puzzle and cross them out. Words may run up, down, forward or backward. When you've found all the names, the remaining letters will tell you what the blue shells make Yoshi do.

SUMO	WIGGLER	NINJI
REZNOR	GOOMBA	MEGA MOLE
URCHIN	SPIKE	SHYGUY
FISH		BOBOMB

H	S	I	F	Y	T	H	B
E	R	E	S	U	M	O	M
R	E	L	G	G	I	W	O
I	Z	O	O	Y	Y	N	B
J	N	M	O	H	S	I	O
N	O	A	M	S	P	H	B
I	R	G	B	M	I	C	A
N	K	E	A	E	K	R	H
I	M	M	F	L	E	U	Y

If you think Mario should smash the yellow shell, turn to page 52.

If you think Mario should smash the blue shell, turn to page 42.

30

"Yoshi will take me there," Mario says. "He likes to eat daisies."

With a leap, Mario jumps onto Yoshi's big toe. Sure enough, after a few moments, the big dinosaur sees the daisies. "Glorp!" He snorts and lumbers toward them. Then he stops and gives a big yawn.

"No!" shouts Mario. "Don't nap now!"

But Yoshi doesn't hear Mario's screams. He lies down on the soft green grass and immediately starts to snore. Mario is trapped under his foot!

"Help!" Mario shouts, trying to pry himself out from under the huge green toes. "Yoshi might sleep for days! I'm helpless! This is worse than being swallowed!"

GAME OVER!

31

"A wrench!" Mario shouts. "Of course! It's a good thing I picked up that toy wrench back there. It ought to do the job."

He pulls out the shiny chrome wrench and twists the valve open. Then he steps through and carefully closes the valve behind him.

"Nothing like a good wrench!" he says happily.

Quickly, he runs down the tunnel and comes out into a large, open space where he almost bumps smack into a huge, green rubber boot.

"Luigi!" Mario shouts at the sight of his brother's big toe.

"About time," Luigi mutters.

Turn to page 6.

32

"Easy," Mario says. "I've got something to shrink you."

"Planning to run him through the dryer?" sneers a nasty, rotten voice.

"Bowser Koopa!" Mario gasps in surprise. The wicked turtle pops his head over Luigi's boot and smiles an evil smile.

"You were expecting maybe Maxi Mushroom and the Mushketeers?" Bowser chortles. "I shrank myself so I could steal that bottle."

Mario places the bottle on the floor of Yoshi's stomach, then turns to face Bowser.

"You'll never get it, you tortoise-shelled turkey!" he cries. "Hurry, Luigi! I'll hold him off! You swallow the shrinking medicine."

"What?" Luigi says from somewhere way above. "Okay, here goes! Ugh! Oof!"

Bowser circles around Mario, trying to get at the bottle.

"Hurry, Luigi!" Mario shouts.

"I'm trying," Luigi answers. "There, I think I've got it!"

Suddenly, Mario feels a gigantic hand close around him.

"Luigi, wait—" he starts to scream, but Luigi's huge fingers close over him. Before he can break free, Luigi has popped him into his mouth and swallowed!

"Okay, Mario, I'm ready to shrink!" Luigi says. "Mario? Mario?"

Turn to page 36.

33

"Drat!" says Mario. "Bowser sure knows how to ruin a party." He turns to the dino doctor. "Doc, can you get Luigi out?"

"*Hmmf!*" says Luigi, from inside Yoshi.

"Don't worry," replies the dino doctor as he rummages around in his bag. He pulls out a very small brown bottle. "The medicine in this bottle will solve everything."

"Great!" sighs Mario. "Well, what are you waiting for? Give it to him!"

"There's only one problem," answers the big duck. "I can't remember who's supposed to take it—Yoshi or Luigi!"

Solve this puzzle to find out who should take the medicine.

- The pictures on the page form a pattern. Who should go next to continue the pattern? That will tell you who should take the medicine.

If you think Yoshi should take the medicine, turn to page 46.

If you think Luigi should take the medicine, turn to page 10.

34

"Wait a minute!" shouts Mario. "There's something funny going on here." He walks over to Fungus Cap. "How come I've never seen you around here before?"

"Maybe you had your head in your plunger," sneers Fungus Cap. He pulls at his mushroom head. It comes off! The turtle face of Bowser Koopa grins at Mario. Fungus Cap is the evil turtle king in disguise!

"I wanted to ruin Yoshi's birthday party," Bowser laughs, "and I think I've done a pretty good job!"

"Snurf!" Yoshi snorts angrily.

"You ain't kidding, Yoshi!" Mario grabs for Bowser's head. But Bowser leaps out of the way, runs to a nearby window and jumps out. Mario is just in time to see the wicked turtle ride off on the back of a Dino-Rhino.

"He got away!" cries Princess Toadstool, who's just behind Mario. "What do we do now?"

"What we should have done in the first place," Mario replies. "Call Doc Drake, the dino doctor!"

Toad goes running out and returns in fifteen minutes with Doc Drake, a four-foot-tall duck.

"What a quack!" whispers the king.

"Very interesting," says the big duck as he peers at Yoshi through his glasses. "Did he by any chance eat a giant purple cherry?"

"Why, yes," answers Mario. "Then he went crazy and ate everything in sight."

"Of course," says Doc Drake. "Because that was no ordinary giant purple cherry. That was a Koopa Cherry. Lucky for you, in addition to being a dino doctor, I also happen to be a Koopologist."

"What's that?" the king whispers to Toad.

"I think it means he's flown the coop," Toad whispers back.

> ***Mario loses 50 points for listening to Fungus Cap.***
> Turn to page 64.

35

"Good thing I remembered the first rule of plumbing," Mario says. "Never leave home without your plunger!"

He dives to the bottom of the pit, fits his plunger over the drain and quickly unclogs it. The punch drains out of the pit.

"Ah!" Mario sighs happily when he's standing on the dry bottom. "Nothing like a good plumbing job to make you feel great!"

He spots a valve on the wall near the bottom of the pit. With a few strong tugs, the valve opens and Mario can crawl into the tunnel on the other side.

"Getting around inside dinosaurs isn't so har—" he starts to say, when the floor tilts under his feet. He slides downward.

"I'm falling!" he yells. "Help!"

Turn to page 76.

36

"Wait a minute!" Mario says as he looks at the shiny, white rock. "That's a tooth! If I'd crawled on top, I'd have been squished flatter than a pizza under a Dino-Rhino!"

Suddenly he's blinded by a light. The big dinosaur is opening his mouth!

"No, Yoshi!" Mario can hear Princess Toadstool yelling. The whole floor starts to tilt and shake. Yoshi is moving.

BOOM! BOOM! Yoshi's steps feel like earthquakes to the tiny plumber.

"Yoshi, stop! Don't drink that!" yells the princess.

A giant wave of purple fruit punch pours in over Yoshi's teeth and knocks Mario off his feet.

"Yeow!" yells Mario as he's swept away by the tide of sticky, purple juice. The flood of punch streams like a waterfall down Yoshi's throat. Mario feels himself falling.

THUD! The plumber bounces against a soft

floor. When he stands up he's knee-deep in grape punch.

"Good thing I'm wearing my hat," he says, and flicks a switch on his red plumber's cap. A bright beam of light shoots out from the front of the cap. Mario sees he's in some kind of large red room with thick rubbery walls.

"Hremp! Frengs!" Luigi's voice vibrates through the walls, but Mario can't tell where it's coming from.

"I'm coming, little brother!" Mario calls. He looks around the bag. There are three narrow tunnels leading out, one on the left, one on the right and one in the middle. Mario pulls on the end of his mustache.

"Which way should I go?" he wonders.

Solve this puzzle to find out something Mario will need if he takes the center tunnel.

• Unscramble the words and write them down. Circle the letters in the unscrambled words that fall in the same place as the circled letters in the scrambled words. Then unscramble the letters you circled. The answer is something Mario will need in the center tunnel.

70

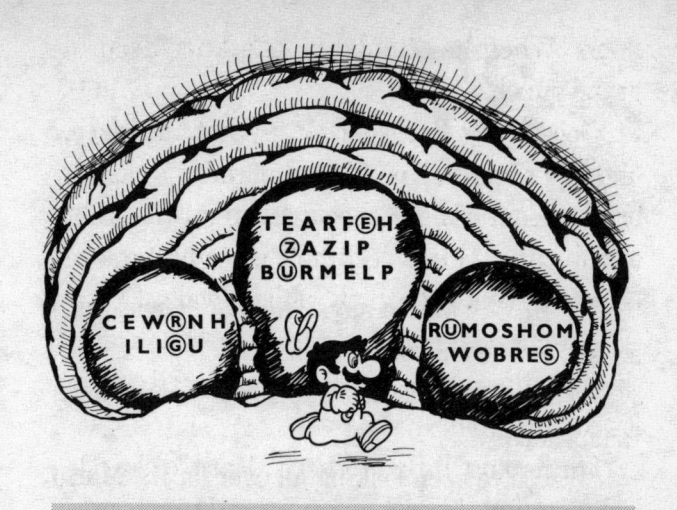

If you think Mario should take the exit on the left, turn to page 20.

If you think Mario should take the exit on the right, turn to page 98.

If you think Mario should take the exit in the center, turn to page 83.

37

"Well..." Mario says slowly. "I was supposed to find this bottle, see...."

"What do you mean, 'supposed?'" Luigi asks suspiciously.

"Well, I've been looking all over for it," Mario snaps huffily. "This is the most disorganized dinosaur I've ever been in! Have you been messing things up in here?"

"No I haven't!" Luigi answers. "When are you going to get me out?"

"I don't know," Mario confesses. "I've looked all over. I must have missed the bottle somewhere along the way. I'll have to climb out and start all over."

Luigi groans. "That'll take forever."

"Don't worry!" Mario says cheerily. "It'll only take almost forever."

GAME OVER!

38

"The platforms are the way to go," says Mario. He hops onto the white rock. But on the next hop, his head hits the rock above.

"Ouch!" he yells. He stares at the white platforms. "Now, where have I seen two rows of white shiny rocks, one above the other?" He rubs his chin and chews on the end of his mustache.

"Ouch!" he says as he pulls on his mustache with his teeth. "Teeth!" he says. "I'm sitting on Yoshi's teeth. Well, I'm certainly glad I . . . TEETH!!??"

Mario jumps up and dives for Yoshi's tongue. But it's too late. The huge teeth come together, pushing him into a crack.

"I'm stuck like a piece of lasagna!" Mario wails as he tries to wriggle out. "Why didn't I bring some dental floss?"

GAME OVER!

39

"Mario, please!" Luigi begs.

"Okay, okay, don't worry," says Mario. Thinking fast, he leaps headfirst at the opposite wall.

Boing!

Mario bounces off the wall like a paper clip off a rubber band.

Boing! Boing! Boing!

The little plumber caroms around the chamber like a cue ball on a pool table. When he finally comes to a halt, he presses his ear to the wall by Luigi's face.

"Mario, what are you doing?" his brother is shouting.

"I thought I'd give Yoshi a stomachache," Mario explains. "Then he wouldn't feel like eating. Did it work?"

"I think so," Luigi grumbles. "But did you have to hit me in the nose four times?"

Solve this puzzle for a clue about what Mario will face next:

• Complete the pattern by writing in the number that should go next. Then go to the start of the path and count off that many letters. Circle the letter you stop on. Keep going until you reach the end of the path. The circled letters spell out a clue.

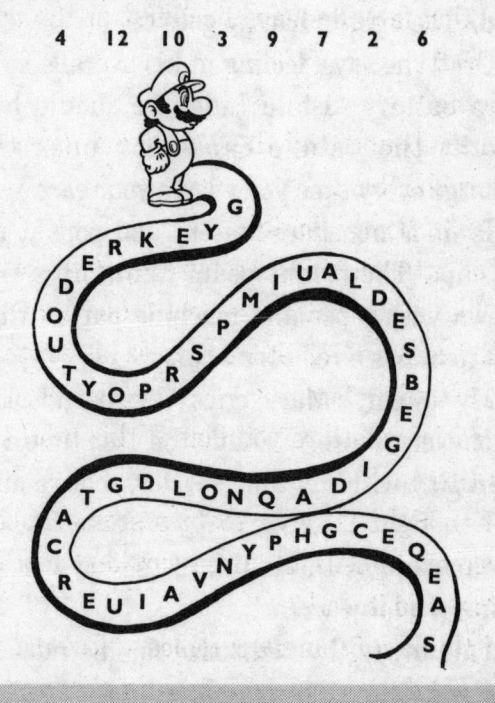

4   12   10   3   9   7   2   6

Turn to page 24.

75

40

B ANG!

With a crash, Mario hits something cold and hard. The light in his cap goes off.

"Drat!" he says, feeling in his overalls for an extra battery. "I told Luigi we should have bought the deluxe caps—the ones that recharge every time you wiggle your ears."

He finds his spare battery and pops it into the cap. The bright beam lights up a floor strewn with pipes and machine parts. Right next to him is a red sports car.

"My toy car!" Mario cries. "I've been looking for it everywhere! That's the last time I let Yoshi play with my things! Hey, that reminds me."

Mario opens the trunk of the toy car and pulls out a large wrench.

"This toy is the right size for me now," he says and hooks the wrench on to his belt. He beams. "Now I feel like a plumber again!"

Using the light from his cap to guide him, Mario steps over the piles of junk and heads for a pipe that seems to lead out of the chamber.

*** Marco now has the wrench.***

Mario gets 100 points for escaping the bugs.

Turn to page 92.

41

"Grab hold, everyone!" Fungus Cap calls as he picks up the end of Yoshi's tail.

"Okay," says Mario. They all grab onto Yoshi and start to push him over.

"Freep!" snorts Yoshi angrily.

"I think he's upset," says the princess.

"What's he griping about?" says Mario. "We have to do all the lifting."

"Glike!" roars Yoshi. He shakes his tail and sends everyone sprawling on the floor.

"Yoshi, wait!" shouts Mario. But the big dinosaur is running across the hall. Before anyone can stop him he's out of the Mushroom Palace and is disappearing down the road.

"There goes Yoshi!" says the princess.

"There goes my brother," moans Mario. "I'll never get Luigi out now!"

GAME OVER!

42

"Luigi!" Mario shouts at one of the lumps in Yoshi's belly. "Find the bottle!"

"Yurmf? Herln?" Luigi answers.

"I can't understand him," Mario groans.

"He's probably got a mouth full of pizza," says Princess Toadstool.

"No, he can't understand us, either," says Mario. "Yoshi's hide is too thick."

"Good news!" shouts Doc Drake.

"You found another birthday cake?" asks the king, running over from the food tables.

"No," answers the dino doctor. "I've got a second bottle of shrink medicine."

"Great," says the princess. "Now, how are we going to get Luigi to swallow it?"

"There's only one thing to do!" Mario declares bravely.

"Call him on the phone?" asks the king.

"No," Mario answers. "This is a job for a super plumber! I'll drink the second bottle of

79

shrink medicine, go inside Yoshi, find the first bottle and bring it to Luigi!"

"I think it would be easier to call him on the phone," says the king.

Princess Toadstool turns to Mario. "You'd better be prepared. What will you take with you?"

"I don't know," Mario answers, pulling on his big, black mustache. "I've never gone inside a dinosaur before. I won't be able to carry much, but I should take one piece of equipment. I've got my plunger here, and my flying suit. Which one should I bring?"

Solve this puzzle to decide what Mario should take with him.

• Each pattern is a code that tells you how to move when you land on it. Start on any one of the four squares in the top row and move according to the pattern that is there. Keep moving until you land on a suit or a plunger.

START

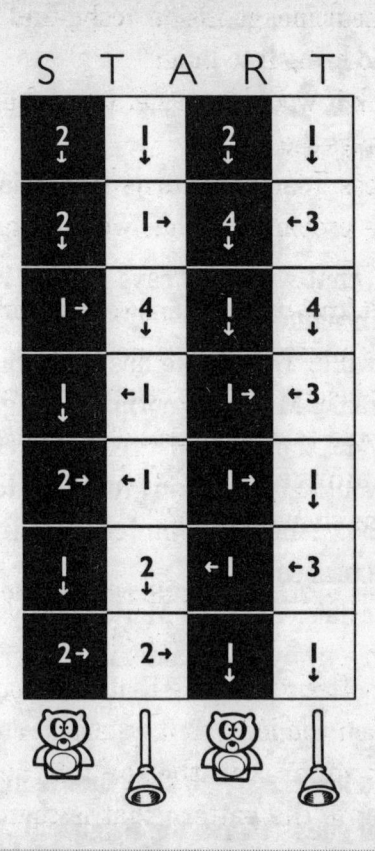

2 ↓	! ↓	2 ↓	! ↓
2 ↓	1 →	4 ↓	← 3
1 →	4 ↓	! ↓	4 ↓
! ↓	← 1	1 →	← 3
2 →	← 1	1 →	! ↓
! ↓	2 ↓	← 1	← 3
2 →	2 →	! ↓	! ↓

Whichever item you land on, mark it on your score sheet.

*** Mario gets 100 points for volunteering to go inside Yoshi.***

Turn to page 112.

81

43

"Well, that was fun," says Mario. He slides off the dinosaur's foot.

Meanwhile, Doc Drake has been thinking of ways to make Mario his normal size again.

"Wait!" he shouts. "I just remembered. Magic daisies would make Mario grow back to his full size. Look, there's a bunch growing right there. I'll pick some!"

"Magic daisies?" says Mario. "They sure are a long way away. It'd take me forever to walk there."

> If Mario has the flying suit, turn to page 17.
> If Mario doesn't have the flying suit, turn to page 60.

44

Mario jumps into the center pipe. *Bonk!* He lands on something wet, covered with thick bristles like the ones on a paintbrush.

"Where am I?" he wonders, trying to untangle himself from the curly black stuff growing all around him. Then he hears a very loud, familiar voice.

"Yuck! Not more food!"

"That's Luigi!" Mario cries. "I must be standing on his head. Hey, little brother!"

"What's that?" Luigi asks, pulling pieces of ravioli out of his ears. "With all this food in my ears, I can't hear a thing. And what's that on my head? A pickle?"

"Pickle!" shouts Mario. "Who are you calling a pickle?"

But Luigi doesn't hear. "This is gross!" he says, and brushes Mario off his head with a swat.

"Yeow!" yells Mario. Before he knows it, he's

falling past Luigi's knees, right into a drain at the bottom of Yoshi's stomach. He's swept away by a tide of grape punch and into a tunnel.

"I'll teach him to call me a pickle," Mario grumbles as he floats along. Then he spots a large pink flower floating nearby. "Look at that," he says. "Yoshi swallowed a flower. I wonder what kind it is?"

Solve this puzzle to find out what kind of flower Yoshi swallowed:

• Cross out every shape with parallel sides. Next, cross out every shape that has more than five sides. The remaining letters tell you the kind of flower Mario has found.

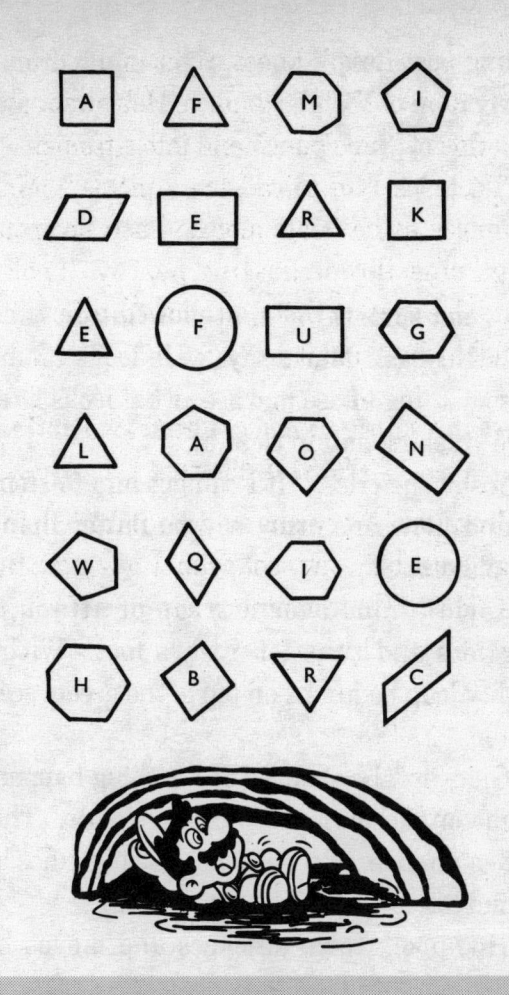

If you think Mario should pick up the flower, mark it on your score sheet.

Turn to page 108.

45

"I need something that can flatten these crazy Koopas!" Mario says. He looks around for something to use and sees what looks like a huge green mountain close by.

"Yoshi!" he cries. "If I can get him to stomp around, Bowser's army will be flatter than a day-old pizza."

Mario jumps over a troop of attacking Wigglers and runs for Yoshi's foot. With a mighty leap he jumps on top of the green, scaly big toe.

"Giddyap!" he shouts. But nothing happens. "Come on, Yoshi, move!" Mario shouts. Then he has an idea. He scratches the big dinosaur behind his curved white claw.

"Hoo-hoo!" Yoshi snickers and moves his foot.

"I knew he was ticklish!" Mario shouts and scratches Yoshi again.

"Hoo-ha!" laughs Yoshi. He starts to hop. *BOOM! BOOM!*

Mario keeps tickling, and Yoshi stomps all over the ground.

"What's gotten into Yoshi?" asks Toad with a worried look.

"I don't know," says the princess, "but I'm worried about Mario."

"Don't worry about me," says tiny Mario. "Ride 'em, cowboy! Yahoo!"

Mega Moles, Dino-Rhinos and Sumo Brothers flee in every direction. Squooshed Wigglers and Koopa Troopas try in vain to hop out of the way. In seconds, Yoshi turns Bowser's army into a mess of mashed meanies.

"I'll get you for this!" shouts Bowser, just before he runs behind a blade of grass and disappears.

Turn to page 82.

46

"Take my advice," insists Fungus Cap. "Don't trust that crazy dino doctor."

"Okay," Mario says. "But we've got to get Luigi out of there."

"Take this, Yoshi," says Fungus Cap. He stuffs a big pink pill into Yoshi's mouth.

From inside Yoshi's stomach they hear Luigi shouting, "PUEGM! KLIPST!"

"What'd he say?" asks Mario.

"He said, 'bounce Yoshi upside down,'" says Fungus Cap.

"It didn't sound like that to me," says Princess Toadstool.

"I don't know," adds Mario. "Yoshi's starting to turn pink. Maybe we should leave him alone."

"Trust me," insists Fungus Cap. "Luigi will come sliding right out! Come on, everyone, help me turn Yoshi upside-down!"

"Should we do it?" the princess asks.

Solve this puzzle to decide if Yoshi should be turned upside-down.

- Answer these questions correctly, then total up your answers. Fill in every space in the puzzle with that number of sides. The picture will show which way Yoshi should be.
- How many cherries did Yoshi eat?
- How many slices of pizza was Luigi carrying at the start of the party?

If you think Yoshi should be turned upside-down, turn to page 78.

If you think Yoshi should stay right side-up, turn to page 66.

47

"Come on, you orange bugs," Mario shouts. "I'm your meatball!"

The orange creatures grab Mario and drag him to the hole in the floor.

"Okay, okay," Mario complains. "Don't push! Hey, watch out! YEOW!"

Crash!

Mario lands on a sticky, moving floor surrounded by piles of food. To Mario, the heaps of spaghetti are as big as fire hoses and the pickles are as large as watermelons.

Breez! Bruzz!

"What is that?" Mario says, turning his cap so the light shines ahead. "Oh, no!" he shouts. "I'm being digested!"

Like a giant conveyor belt, the moving floor is carrying him straight toward a large opening. Mario stares in horror as he sees the walls of the opening crash and rub together, grinding the food into tiny pieces.

"That's dangerous," he says. "And disgusting, too! Let me outta here!"

Overhead, Mario spots an opening. He reaches up for it, but slips on a wet hunk of cheese. By the time he gets up, he's even closer to the grinding walls.

"I've heard of food processors, but this is ridiculous!" Mario says and starts running. He slips again and falls face first into a pile of rice pudding, jumps up and leaps over an olive, hurdles a pretzel as big as a tree trunk, and with a final jump grabs the opening of the pipe and hauls himself in.

Mario loses 100 points for almost getting digested.

Turn to page 92.

48

Mario crawls through the pipe and after a while pokes his head into another large chamber. This one has purplish walls that are curved and bent in strange shapes.

"Hremf? Clredg?"

"Luigi!" Mario says as his brother's muffled voice echoes through the room. "Where are you, little brother?"

"Marmb? Gedoya!"

Mario turns his searchlight all around the dark chamber, but he can't see a sign of Luigi. He sits down and looks at the strangely-shaped wall.

"I know I've seen that wall before," he says. "But where?"

"Marim! Whereya!"

As Luigi's voice booms through the room, Mario sees the whole wall move.

"It's him!" Mario shouts, jumping up. "Luigi's on the other side of that wall!"

Mario presses his ear to the rubbery wall and suddenly he can hear Luigi clearly.

"That Mario!" Luigi is saying. "I wish he'd hurry up and get me out of here. And I wish Yoshi'd quit drinking grapeade! Yuck!"

Mario presses his face to the wall. "Luigi!" he shouts. "Can you hear me?"

"Mario? Mario, where are you?"

"I'm on the other side of the wall," Mario answers. "Just above your left nostril, I think."

"Well, could you move?" Luigi says. "You're making my nose itch! How'd you get in here, anyway?"

Quickly, Mario explains how Doc Drake shrank him so he could rescue Luigi.

"Great," says Luigi. "Now if the princess could only get Yoshi to stop eating for a while. Every time he opens his mouth a new load of food lands on my head."

BOOM! BOOM!

"What's happening?" Mario yells, as everything around him starts to shake.

"I think Yoshi is moving," Luigi answers. "When he opens his mouth I can hear people talking outside. Listen!"

Mario presses his ear to the wall and hears Princess Toadstool's voice.

"Yoshi! Stop!" she's saying angrily. "Don't go down those stairs! YOSHI!"

BOOM, BOOM, BOOM, BOOM!

Mario is thrown from one end of the chamber to the other. Luckily, the walls are soft. He climbs back to Luigi and presses his ear to the wall again.

"Mario, you're standing on my eyeball," Luigi complains.

"Sorry," says Mario. "What's happening now?"

"I think we're outside, in the palace garden," Luigi answers. "Listen!"

"Yoshi, stop right there," Princess Toadstool is saying. "No, you can't eat those boomer berries. YOSHI!"

"Not boomer berries," wails Luigi. "They smell worse than three-day-old sauerkaut. Mario, do something!"

"Like what?" Mario asks.

Solve this puzzle to help decide what Mario should do.

• Answer the questions to come up with a number. Then, starting with the first letter of the coded message, move forward or backward

94

in the alphabet the number of letters equal to that number. Write down the new letter. Do this for each letter of the message. The decoded message is a clue for Mario.

- The number of letters in the color of Mario's plumber's uniform is ___.
- Add the number of ducks Mario has seen so far in this adventure, which is ___.
- Subtract the number of pieces of cake Luigi ate before Yoshi swallowed him, which is ___.
- Use the total to decode this message:

WQIPPC FIVVMIW EVI SOEC

If you think Mario should stop Yoshi, turn to page 74.

If you think Mario shouldn't stop Yoshi, turn to page 54.

49

S<small>QUOOSH!</small>

Mario lands on top of a Wiggler.

"I must have something I can use to fight these creeps," he says.

Meanwhile, Princess Toadstool, Luigi and the others are looking for him.

"MARIO!" The princess's voice sounds like an explosion to tiny Mario. "WHERE ARE YOU?"

"How can he tell us?" asks Toad. "He's too small for us to hear."

"Maybe he can send up a smoke signal," says the king.

"Smoke!" says Mario, smashing a mini-Ninji. "How am I going to send up a smoke signal without any fire? Fire? Hey, wait a minute...."

Mario pulls out the flower he found inside Yoshi. "I knew this looked familiar," he says. "It's a fireflower!"

Mario grasps the fireflower and ...

WHOOSH!

A large orange fireball comes shooting out. It flies into Bowser's army and explodes, knocking over three dozen Shyguys.

"Hey!" shouts Bowser. "No fair!"

"Too bad, tortoise-face!" Mario shoots a fireball right at Bowser.

"Yeow!" Bowser screams and runs for cover behind a blade of grass.

"Look," says Doc Drake, who is a few feet away, peering at a flower. "I think I found something that can make Mario full-size again. These magic daisies should do the trick. All he has to do is bite one of the petals. I'll bring him some."

"NO!" shouts the Princess. "Don't move! With those big webbed feet, you'll probably step on him. No, Mario will have to reach the daisies by himself."

Mario gains 100 points for stopping Bowser's army.

Turn to page 47.

50

Mario climbs into the right-hand pipe. The floor slopes down and he hops along quickly. Soon he finds himself in a large cavern with green spikes on the floor and ceiling. A faint green light shines through the roof.

"This must be Yoshi's back," Mario says. "I can see sunlight through his scales. Boy, they're dirty—I've got to get him to bathe."

The floor of the cavern is sickly brown, with large patches of gray fungus growing all over the place. Mario thinks he sees a way out on the far side of the chamber.

That's the way I want to go," he says. "I don't know if I should walk on the brown stuff. It looks kind of gooey. Those gray patches don't look much better, though."

Solve this puzzle to help you decide where Mario should walk.

- Mario has to find a path through the cavern,

but he has to follow these two rules: His path must be a straight line, and there must be more fungus spots than brown patches on each side of his path. He can start anywhere along the top, and the path must reach the bottom. The path cannot go through a fungus spot or a brown patch. Can he do it?

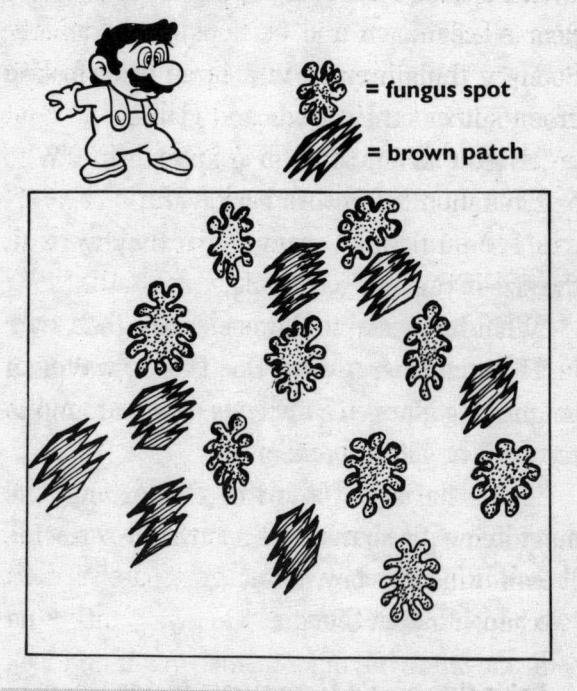

= fungus spot

= brown patch

**If you think Mario can't do it, turn to page 40.
If you think Mario can do it, turn to page 18.**

51

"Well, aren't you going to thank me?" Mario says to Luigi.

"Hah!" Luigi says. "While you were fooling around, it was the doc who saved me."

"Fooling around?" Mario splutters. "Who had to fight all of Bowser's army?"

"I could fight an army too, if they were all the size of raisins," says Luigi.

"What happened to Bowser?" asks Toad.

"He's right here," says Doc Drake, waving a magnifying glass. The friends crowd around to see what he's looking at.

"There he is!" shouts Luigi. Through the magnifying glass, they see a tiny Bowser being chased by a large brown ant.

"Help!" Bowser shouts. "Go away, ant! Find someone who's having a picnic! What do I look like, a bread crumb?"

"Ha!" Mario laughs. "I always said Bowser was small-minded."

"Well, Luigi and Mario," says Princess Toadstool. "Now that you're back to normal, what do you want to do for the rest of the afternoon?"

"I'm going back to the party," declares the king. "Maybe my loyal subjects haven't eaten all of the cake."

"Plorp!" Yoshi says eagerly.

"Good idea," says Doc Drake. "By the way, who do I send my bill to?"

"That duck always has a big bill," Toad whispers.

"What about you two?" the princess asks the plumbers. "Want to go back to the party?"

"You bet," says Luigi. "My stomach is rumbling and it's not Mario talking to me."

"I'm not hungry," says Mario, looking a little green. "In fact, after what I've been through, I may never eat again! Luigi, haven't you done enough eating today?"

"No way!" says Luigi. "You know me, eating always helps me work up an appetite!"

GAME OVER. YOU WIN!

52

"Too bad I didn't bring my plunger," Mario says. He swims around the edge of the pit again, looking for a way to climb up. The walls are wet and slippery and he can't find anyplace to pull himself up.

"Maybe I can use my flying suit," Mario muses. He pulls the suit out of his pocket. But the roaring punch waterfall grabs it from his hands and carries it away before he even knows what's happening.

"What am I going to do now?" he moans, swimming in circles. "I may have to swim around inside Yoshi forever. It's all my fault for forgetting the first rule of plumbing: never leave home without your plunger!"

GAME OVER!

53

SPLAT! Bowser slugs Mario with an anchovy the size of a bath towel.

"Let him eat!" Mario shouts. "No matter what happens, it can't be worse than this!"

"Okay," Luigi says. "Hold on, Mario!"

Suddenly everything starts to vibrate. Yoshi starts to shake. Luigi shakes around inside of Yoshi. Mario and Bowser shake around inside of Luigi.

"What's happening?" Luigi shouts.

"What's happening?" Mario shouts.

"Just what I need, stereo plumbers," Bowser mutters.

For a moment, all is still. Then ...
PTUI!
Yoshi spits out Luigi! He goes flying through the air and lands on a soft patch of grass. He's on a hill just outside the palace, surrounded by the princess, Toad, the king, the dino doctor and Yoshi.

"Luigi!" cries Princess Toadstool.

"I knew it would work!" says Doc Drake. "At least I thought I knew."

"Plorp!" says Yoshi, rubbing his stomach.

"But where's Mario?" asks the princess.

Luigi looks embarrassed. "I swallowed him by mistake. We've got to get him out."

"Let him stay where he is," suggests the king. "Isn't one plumber enough?"

"Eat these," says Doc Drake and hands Luigi some threelip petals.

Luigi munches on them. "Hmm, with a little parmesan, they'd be okay," he says. Suddenly he starts to shake. Then . . .

PTUI!

"I don't see Mario!" cries Toad.

"He's too small," says Doc Drake.

"Nobody move!" shouts the princess. "We don't want to squash him! Quick, Doctor, make him his normal size."

"What do you mean?" the big duck asks.

"You can make him normal-sized again, can't you?" says the princess.

"Uh, I don't know," says the dino doctor, rubbing his bill. "I think so."

Solve this puzzle to find out what Mario needs to get bigger.

• Get the princesss through the maze without stepping on Mario. If she steps on the stones in the right order, the letters she steps on will spell out something Mario's going to need.

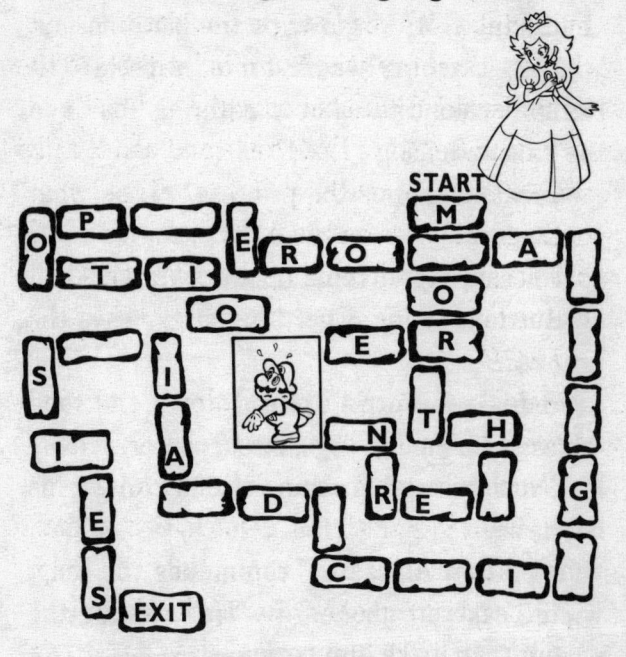

Mario gets 100 points for getting out of Luigi.

Turn to page 26.

54

Thinking fast, Mario trips the big dinosaur, who goes crashing headfirst into the table. The birthday cake topples over, covering Toad and the king with icing.

"Great!" exclaims the princess. "Look what you've done!"

"You said to stop him," answers Mario.

"But he's eating everything else!" says the princess.

Yoshi is running up and down the food tables, gobbling hot dogs, pizza, popcorn, ravioli sandwiches and anything else he can get his hands on.

"Stop that dinosaur!" commands the king, wiping cake off his beard. "He's ruining the party!"

"It must have been that cherry," says the princess. "It's making him eat everything in sight."

"I am not eating everything in sight!" says

Luigi, who walks over, holding a steaming bowl of artichoke lasagna. "I didn't even touch the onion dip."

"Not you!" Mario yells. "It's Yoshi!"

"Maybe he's hungry." Luigi shrugs. "After all, he's a growing dinosaur."

Luigi realizes he forgot the parmesan cheese. He turns back to the table just as Yoshi finishes draining a 50-gallon punch bowl of green fizz. Yoshi looks down and sees Luigi. He opens his gigantic mouth and swallows the plumber in one gulp!

"Luigi!" shout Mario and the princess together.

"Oorp!" says Yoshi.

Turn to page 29.

55

Mario floats along on the stream of grape punch.

"At least this is restful," he sighs, floating on his back and as the gray and green polka-dot ceiling passes by. "I wonder what that noise is? Kind of reminds me of the time Luigi and I went to the Buttermilk Falls... Falls? Oh, no!"

Before he can do anything, Mario roars over a grape punch waterfall and splashes down in a deep pool of the sweet-smelling stuff.

"I should've brought my frog suit," he mutters as he swims around looking for a way out. But he can't find any.

"There's one place I haven't looked," he says. Taking a deep breath, he dives to the bottom. By the beam of his headlight he sees something that looks like a drain, but it's clogged with a tangled mess of food.

"Phew!" he gasps as he comes to the surface.

"Yoshi's plumbing sure is a mess. It'd take a plunger to unclog that drain."

> **If Mario has the plunger, turn to page 68.**
> **If Mario doesn't have the plunger, turn to page 102.**

56

"Send for Doc Drake," says Mario.

"You're making a mistake," says Fungus Cap.

In ten minutes Toad returns with the dino doctor. The giant mallard waddles up on bright yellow webbed feet and peers at Yoshi through his glasses. The big dinosaur is green again, and seems normal, except for the Luigi-shaped bulge in his belly.

"Aha!" exclaims Doc Drake.

"What is it, doctor?" asks the princess.

"Your highness," the dino doctor declares. "I've found the problem. This dinosaur has a plumber in his stomach!"

"Some doctor," sneers Fungus Cap.

"Can you get him out?" Mario pleads.

"Of course," the duck answers calmly. "I've treated many cases like this. Did he by any chance eat a giant purple cherry?"

"Why, yes," answers Mario.

"Ah!" says Doc Drake. "That was no ordinary giant purple cherry. It was a Koopa Cherry, from the garden of that no-goodnik, Bowser Koopa. Who put it on the cake?"

Toad steps forward. "I did," he says. "Fungus Cap gave it to me!"

"You!" exclaims Mario, glaring at Fungus Cap. "Who are you, anyway?"

"Who do you think, you pitiful plumber!" Fungus Cap pulls at his round mushroom head and it comes off, revealing the leering, warty green face of Bowser Koopa! Fungus Cap is really the evil king of the turtles!

"I planned to ruin Yoshi's party," laughs the turtle. "But this is better than I'd hoped. Say hi to Luigi for me—if you ever see him again!"

Before Mario can stop him, Bowser jumps out a window and lands on top of a waiting Dino-Rhino. Ten coins fly out of his pocket.

"Hi-ho!" he shouts and gallops away.

"I'll get him for this!" Mario yells.

Mario collects 10 coins for unmasking Bowser.
Turn to page 64.

57

"Mario, be careful in there," says Princess Toadstool.

"I'll be fine," says Mario. "Just make sure Yoshi doesn't eat anything else. I don't want to wind up swimming in a sea of spaghetti sauce."

"Sounds like fun to me," says the king.

Mario lifts the bottle to his lips. "I'll be back!" he vows. "With Luigi!"

"Wait!" says Toad. "While you're in there, what do we do? What about all the other guests?"

Mario looks at the hundreds of loyal mushroom subjects who have gathered around. Then he spies the orange and green pile of goo that is the remains of Yoshi's birthday cake.

"Let them eat cake!" Mario says grandly, and swallows the medicine.

Whoosh!

Mario feels the air rushing by as, suddenly, he shrinks until he's just a fraction of an inch high.

"Yow!" he shouts. "What's that!?"

Mario thinks a giant pink mountain is about to fall on him. Then he realizes it's the hand of Princess Toadstool, reaching down to lift him into Yoshi's mouth.

"MARIO!! ARE YOU OKAY??"

The roar of Princess Toadstool's voice almost knocks the plumber over.

Swoosh!

The princess grabs him by his red overalls and lifts him through the air. To the tiny Mario, it seems as if he's soaring a hundred miles above the ground. Suddenly he's hanging upside-down above a giant, dark cavern lined with rows of sharp white rocks.

That's no cavern," he says to himself. "That's Yoshi's mouth! Maybe this wasn't such a good idea. Hey, Princess!" he shouts. "Put me down!"

The princess hears Mario squeaking.

"He's so brave," she says to Toad and the king, wiping a tear from her eye. Then she lets go of Mario's overalls.

"Watch out below!" Mario yells as he plunges down.

He lands with a soft thud on Yoshi's large,

113

pink tongue. He tries to stand up, but the tongue is too wet and slippery. He scrambles toward a smooth, hard white area.

"That's a relief," he gasps, holding onto the shiny white platform. He looks directly above his head. "Hmm," he says, "there's another one up there. It reminds me of something."

He sees another white platform next to the one he's on, and beyond that another. Like giant white stepping stones, they lead back into Yoshi's mouth. "These platforms seem to lead somewhere," he thinks. "Maybe I should follow them."

Solve this puzzle for a hint about something Mario will need if he stays where he is.

• Mario can jump from one stepping stone to another. He can move forward and sidewise, but not diagonally or backwards. As you pass over the letters, write them down. If you find the correct way to Luigi, then the letters will spell the name of an item Mario might use.

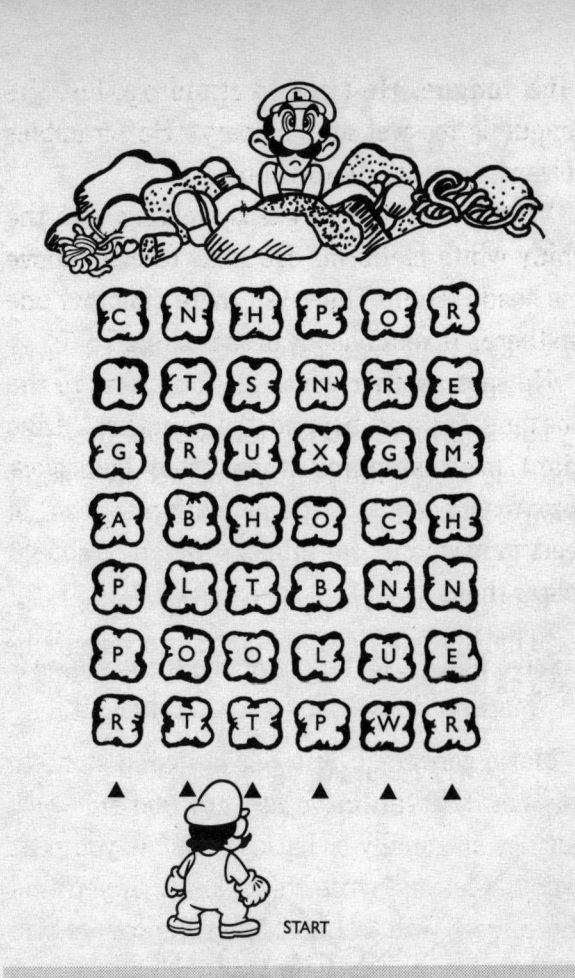

If you think Mario should follow the platforms, turn to page 73.

If you think Mario should go back onto Yoshi's tongue, turn to page 69.

58

"Okay, you crazy blue bugs," Mario says. "You win!"

Holding his nose, he jumps boots-first into the hole where the gurgling noises are coming from.

"YEOW!"

He slides down a steep, twisting chute.

"That's what I get for talking to bugs," he says as he falls.

Turn to page 76.

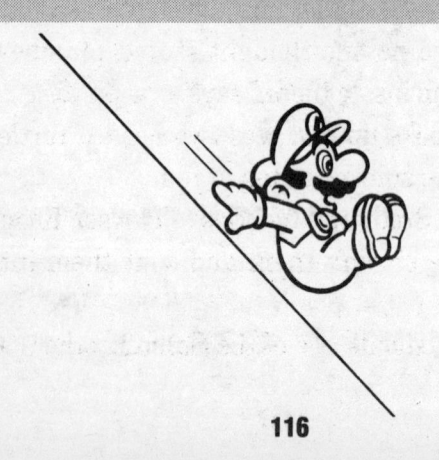

59

"I'd better try to reach Luigi," Mario says. "Sounds like he's in trouble."

He struggles up the inside of Yoshi's tail, listening for any sign of a hiccough. When one comes, he lies down and grabs hold of the thick green carpet.

After a while, the hiccoughing stops and Mario makes his way up the long tail until he comes to a sloping tunnel that leads up.

"This must be the way," he says, lugging the bottle up the steep hill. "Why don't they make dinosaurs with escalators?"

"Because no one thought stupid plumbers would climb inside them," says a raspy voice.

Mario looks up and sees two hooded turtles in one-piece suits charging at him.

"Sumo Brothers!" he cries. "Bowser Koopa must have shrunk them and sent them into Yoshi!"

"Bingo!" shouts one of the Sumo Brothers as

he charges right into Mario and knocks him flat. It's all Mario can do to hold onto the bottle.

"Nobody knocks over a Super Mario Brother!" Mario shouts.

"Oh, yeah?" sneers the other Sumo Brother. He charges into Mario from the other side, sending him flying.

"Well," Mario fumes, "nobody knocks over a Super Mario Brother twice!" He carefully puts down the bottle and turns to face the two Koopa commandos.

> ***Mario gets 100 points for leaving Yoshi's tail.***
> **Turn to page 57.**

60

"Yee-ha!" Mario shouts as he rides on Donny's back. "Ride 'em, cowboy!"

The micro-dolphins laugh again. "What a comedian. First dinosaurs, now cows," Donny says. "Everyone knows cows are extinct!"

Donny and his pals cross the lake with no problem—the sticky Kola just slides off them. Before long, Mario is standing on the other shore, wiping Koopa Kola off his boots.

"Thanks a lot," he says as the micro-dolphins turn to swim away.

"Don't mention it," Donny answers. "Say hi to the dinosaur when you see him. Ha, ha!"

"I guess I wouldn't believe me either," Mario says. He turns away from the lake and comes face to face with a high yellow cliff.

The wall stretches as far as Mario can see in either direction. A narrow staircase leads up one side. He starts to bounce up the stairs.

KABOOM!

A shell from a Koopa Troopa explodes just above him. Mario looks up and sees an entire army of Koopa commandos coming down the staircase at him!

"I can't get past them," he says, looking at the narrow stairs. "And there are too many of them for me to fight. I sure could use some help."

> **If Mario has the Starman, turn to page 5.**
> **If Mario doesn't have the Starman, turn to page 16.**

Drip by Drip Scorecard

Circle each object as you collect it.

Keep track of your score here:

105

Now, use this chart to find your PPR (Personal Plumber Rating) for this adventure. Score ten points for every coin Mario has at the end of the story, and add that to your total. Then look up your rating on this chart.

Did you play hopscotch with the fungus? Did you figure out which color Koopa shell to smash? Did you ride on the micro-dolphins? Read the book again and see if you can increase your score.

- 1201 or more ← Perfect Plumber
- Dinosaur Explorer → 801 to 1200
- 501 to 800 ← Stomach Surveyor
- Plunger Pupil → 201 to 500
- 200 or less ← Leaky Gasket

A Selected List of Fiction from Mammoth

While every effort is made to keep prices low, it is sometimes necessary to increase prices at short notice. Mandarin Paperbacks reserves the right to show new retail prices on covers which may differ from those previously advertised in the text or elsewhere.

The prices shown below were correct at the time of going to press.

☐	7497 0978 2	**Trial of Anna Cotman**	Vivien Alcock £2.50
☐	7497 0712 7	**Under the Enchanter**	Nina Beachcroft £2.50
☐	7497 0106 4	**Rescuing Gloria**	Gillian Cross £2.50
☐	7497 0035 1	**The Animals of Farthing Wood**	Colin Dann £3.50
☐	7497 0613 9	**The Cuckoo Plant**	Adam Ford £3.50
☐	7497 0443 8	**Fast From the Gate**	Michael Hardcastle £1.99
☐	7497 0136 6	**I Am David**	Anne Holm £2.99
☐	7497 0295 8	**First Term**	Mary Hooper £2.99
☐	7497 0033 5	**Lives of Christopher Chant**	Diana Wynne Jones £2.99
☐	7497 0601 5	**The Revenge of Samuel Stokes**	Penelope Lively £2.99
☐	7497 0344 X	**The Haunting**	Margaret Mahy £2.99
☐	7497 0537 X	**Why The Whales Came**	Michael Morpurgo £2.99
☐	7497 0831 X	**The Snow Spider**	Jenny Nimmo £2.99
☐	7497 0992 8	**My Friend Flicka**	Mary O'Hara £2.99
☐	7497 0525 6	**The Message**	Judith O'Neill £2.99
☐	7497 0410 1	**Space Demons**	Gillian Rubinstein £2.50
☐	7497 0151 X	**The Flawed Glass**	Ian Strachan £2.99

All these books are available at your bookshop or newsagent, or can be ordered direct from the publisher. Just tick the titles you want and fill in the form below.

Mandarin Paperbacks, Cash Sales Department, PO Box 11, Falmouth, Cornwall TR10 9EN.

Please send cheque or postal order, no currency, for purchase price quoted and allow the following for postage and packing:

UK including BFPO   £1.00 for the first book, 50p for the second and 30p for each additional book ordered to a maximum charge of £3.00.

Overseas including Eire   £2 for the first book, £1.00 for the second and 50p for each additional book thereafter.

NAME (Block letters) ....

ADDRESS ....

....

☐ I enclose my remittance for ....

☐ I wish to pay by Access/Visa Card Number

Expiry Date